Symphony for the Geese
Written by Tommy Watkins

Four geese were swimming
in a pond on a starry night.

The night was peaceful at the pond.

Storm clouds started to roll in.

Thunder and lightning erupted in the night sky.

A coyote stormed the pond
to threaten the geese.

The geese were frightened
by the vicious coyote.

The coyote paced the shore, ready to pounce on the geese.

The four geese created
a united front against the coyote.

The storm clouds cleared,
and the coyote ran away into the dark
of the night.
The night became peaceful.

The End